Contents

 Fiction

Chased
page 2

 Non-fiction

Space Travel
page 18

Written by
David Clayton
Illustrated by
Peter Richardson

Series editor **Dee Reid**

Heinemann

Part of Pearson

Characters

Joe

Man in a silver suit

Man in a dark suit

Tricky words

- restricted
- followed
- another
- surprised

- intruder
- appeared
- notice
- shoved

Read these words to the student. Help them with these words when they appear in the text.

Introduction

Joe was on the Moon tube. He knew there was something strange going on in Moon City but he didn't know what. He heard a lady say 'Restricted Red Zone' on her video phone and he decided to follow her. He took a lift to a tunnel deep down below Moon City. He sneaked inside a room and saw a huge screen. What Joe saw on the screen made his heart thump.

Chased

Joe was on the Moon tube. He was trying to work things out. Something strange was going on in Moon City, but he didn't know what.

Next to him a lady was talking on her video phone. Joe heard the words 'Restricted Red Zone'.

I'm going to follow her, thought Joe. *This is my chance to find out what is going on.*

When the lady got off at a stop, Joe got off too. He followed the lady but kept out of sight. He saw her use a red swipe card to call a lift.

How can I get into the lift without her seeing me? Joe thought.

Just then, the lift doors opened and some people got out. They stopped to talk to the lady. *This is my chance*, thought Joe and he slipped behind the people and into the lift.

They were still talking as the lift doors closed and the lift took Joe down.

The lift went down a long way. When it stopped, Joe got out. He was in a dark tunnel.

This must be below the Moon City tube tunnel, he thought. *But it seems too far down to be the workers' tunnel. What goes on here?*

He saw a ladder on the wall but he couldn't see where it went up to.

Just then, he heard another lift coming down. He hid in the shadows and watched a man get out of the lift and walk down the tunnel.

I've got to find out what's going on!
thought Joe, so he followed the man.
The man opened a big steel door and
went inside. Quickly, Joe sneaked inside too.

The man went over to a computer.
Joe stood by the door and looked around.
Wow! he thought, *What's all this?*
There was a huge screen on the wall.
On the screen was a map of Earth.

The cities around the world were marked
by red lights. Each city had a number on it.
On New York it said 'Target I'.

Joe was so surprised that he let the door slam shut. BANG!

The man spun round from his computer.
"We've got an intruder!" he shouted, "GET HIM!"
In a split second, other men in silver suits appeared
and ran towards Joe.

Quickly, Joe opened the door. He ran out of the room, slamming the door shut behind him. *RUN!* he thought. He charged back down the tunnel.

He came to the ladder going up through the roof. *If they catch up with me, I'm dead*, he thought. He began to climb the ladder as fast as he could.

He could hear the men's heavy boots on the ladder below him. They were getting closer and closer. He looked down. One man was just behind him. Joe kicked him as hard as he could. Joe heard a sharp cry of pain and the man fell down on to the others below him.

Joe's heart was thumping.
How am I going to get out? he thought.
When he got to the top of the ladder he
saw he was in another tunnel.
Now which way? he thought.

A group of men were coming along the tunnel.
They looked like Moon City tube workers.
They must be going off shift, Joe thought.
He joined the group. They were going to
the lift so Joe got in the lift with them.
He hoped the workers wouldn't notice him.

They came out of the lift into a Moon tube
station. As Joe walked up to street level he saw
a group of men standing by the barriers.
One of them had a smashed and bloody nose.
He was looking for Joe.

Just then Joe felt a heavy hand on his shoulder.
This is it, thought Joe.
But he turned to see a man in a dark suit.
The man grabbed Joe's arm and shoved him
through a door, away from the waiting men.
"Keep away from here," hissed the man, then he
was gone.

Joe's mind was buzzing. *What was going
on in those secret tunnels and who was
the man in the dark suit?*
Joe knew that something very strange was
going on deep below Moon City.

Quiz ///////////////////////////

Text comprehension

Literal comprehension
p5 How did Joe get into the lift without anyone noticing?
p9 How did the man in the silver suit know that Joe was in the room?

Inferential comprehension
p4 Why did Joe follow the lady on the Moon tube?
p13 How can we tell that Joe is scared?
p15 Why was the man with the smashed and bloody nose looking for Joe?

Personal response
- Would you have followed the woman with the video phone?
- What would you want to ask the man in the dark suit?

Word knowledge

p9 Find a word that means 'shocked'.
p10 Why are the words "GET HIM!" in capital letters?
p12 Find two adjectives on this page.

Spelling challenge

Read these words:

another   surprised   wouldn't

Now try to spell them!

Ha! Ha! Ha!

What did one lift say to the other lift?

I think I'm coming down with something!

Find out about

- the race between the Americans and the Russians to get a human into space.

Tricky words

- scientists
- decided
- Yuri Gagarin
- disaster
- astronauts
- parachute
- international
- exciting

Read these words to the student. Help them with these words when they appear in the text

Introduction

Before people travelled in Space, scientists sent animals into Space to see if they could survive. When scientists thought it was safe for people to travel into Space, the space race between America and Russia began. The Russian, Yuri Gagarin, was the first man in Space.

Space Travel

Animals in Space

In the 1950s, scientists in America and Russia wanted to know if it was safe for people to travel into Space.
The scientists decided to send animals up into Space to see if they could survive.

The Americans sent a monkey into Space
in a rocket. The monkey was called Albert.
Sadly, Albert died.
Then the Russians sent a dog called Laika
into Space. Sadly, Laika died too.

Then in 1960, the Russians sent two dogs up into Space. The dogs came back alive.
Then the scientists knew it was safe for people to travel into Space.

The Space Race

The Americans and the Russians started a race to see who would be the first to get a human into Space. The Americans thought they would be first. But they were wrong.
In 1961, Yuri Gagarin, a Russian pilot, went into Space and flew around the Earth.

The next step in the space race was to land a man on the Moon. But this was not easy and sadly some missions into Space ended in disaster.

In 1967, the American spacecraft Apollo I caught fire and three astronauts were killed. In the same year, a Russian astronaut died when his spacecraft's parachute didn't open.

Landing on the Moon

In 1969, two Americans, Neil Armstrong and Buzz Aldrin made it to the Moon.
But even this trip was almost a disaster!
They nearly landed on rocks and then they almost ran out of fuel. But in the end they landed on the Moon.
The whole world watched it on TV.
As Neil Armstrong stepped down on to the Moon he said, "One small step for man, one giant leap for mankind."

LIVE FROM THE MOON

Space Stations

Some trips into Space are short, but some trips can last for weeks or months.
Some astronauts go into Space to live in space stations which fly around in Space.

In the 1990s, Russians and Americans decided to build a space station together. It is called the International Space Station.

Astronauts from around the world work together in the Space Station. They are usually there for six months at a time. And it's not just men! Women astronauts work in the International Space Station too.

Vomit Comets

Have you ever been on a ride
at a theme park where you
drop down suddenly from very
high up?
Did it make you feel sick?
This is how you might feel if
you went into Space.

In Space there is very little gravity.
This is why things float around.
Astronauts prepare for this by going
in special planes which fly up very
high and then fly down really fast.
For a few minutes they float as if they
were in Space. However, this often
makes the astronauts sick. That's why
they called the planes 'vomit comets'.

Living in Space

Living in Space might seem exciting but it is not all fun. How would you like to live with the same people in a space no bigger than a school corridor for six months? It is like being kept in your house for hundreds of days at a time and not being able to go out.

Many astronauts feel sick on their way into Space, and many people in space stations feel dizzy all the time. This is because there is little gravity to pull their blood to their feet.

The food that astronauts take into Space is not the same as on Earth. Food or drink can damage the space station if it floats around, so it has to be eaten very carefully. The first space meals were mushy foods that astronauts squeezed into their mouths from tubes.

Today, scientists are able to make the astronauts' favourite foods for them to eat in Space. They put the food in small packets. The astronauts have to add water to the packets before they can eat the meal.

Going to the toilet in Space is also different from Earth. The toilet fits tightly round your body. When you have used the toilet, the waste is sucked away into storage bags.
But the first Space toilets didn't work properly for female astronauts! So Space travel might not be as exciting as you might think!

Quiz ////////////////////

Text comprehension

Literal comprehension
p22 Who was the first person in Space?
p24 Why was the first landing on the Moon nearly a disaster?

Inferential comprehension
p27 Why do you think the Space Station is International?
p28 Why are astronauts sent in the vomit comets?
p29/31 Why might space travel not always be very exciting?

Personal response
- Do you think it was fair to send animals into Space to test safety?
- Would you like to go to the International Space Station?

Word knowledge

p24 Find two words which are opposite in meaning, in the words spoken by Neil Armstrong.
p27 Why is there an exclamation mark after the word 'men'?
p30 Which word describes the first space food?

Spelling challenge

Read these words:

brought   minutes   somebody

Now try to spell them!

Ha! Ha! Ha!

When do astronauts have lunch?

At launch time!